CONTEMPORARY ANGST

POEMS
DAVID K. WAGNER

Copyright © 2024 Dave Wagner

Published by CaryPress International Books

www.CaryPress.com

All rights reserved. No part of this publication may be reproduced, distributed, or transmitted in any form or by any means, including photocopying, recording, or other electronic or mechanical methods, without the prior written permission of the publisher, except in the case of brief quotations embodied in critical reviews and certain other non-commercial uses permitted by copyright law.

CONTEMPORARY ANGST

David Wagner was born in Pittsburgh, Pennsylvania. His father, a WWII veteran, worked in packing houses and drove heavy trucks before retiring from job injuries. David is from a family of five children. He studied at Virginia Tech, before moving to Charlotte, North Carolina where he maintained a career as an Architect for fifty years. Pursuits included graphic design, art, furniture design, product design and related fields. Writing, largely commentary led to composing poetry. Recognized as a thought leader in his field he continues to stay active in community work outside his practice. This is his first collection of poetry.

I turn onto my back.
All of me is lifted at once,
as if it were impossible to drown.

Raymond Carver

Early work is suspect, and will be used as a sort of graph which charts one's progress and can be imagined as a minor mistake. It can be used to associate the writer with his own history, rather than his own heart.

Harry Golden writing on Carl Sandburg

Cover illustration by David K. Wagner

DAVID K. WAGNER

CONTEMPORARY ANGST

POEMS

CONTENTS
POEMS | ONE

WHAT AM I MISSING?	2
AWE AND WONDER	4
TRAFFIC	5
DOUBT	6
DELAY	7
MEASURING WITH A NEW SET OF RULES	8
CARDIAC REPERCUSSIONS	10
ONE GLASS OR THREE	11
EV MANDATE	12
LET'S START WITH THINGS THAT BOTHER YOU	14
ENERGY	15
THE BAKERY LINE	17
A SHORT TRIP	18
HEAT	19
ARISE AND REFLECT	20
DECIPHERING THE CHATTER	21
WAR DEBT	22
NEWS	24
SO LONG FRANK LIOYD WRIGHT	26
SKY	28
THINKING ABOUT ANXIETY	29
CHILDHOOD	30
BOOKS	31
STATE OF THE WORLD	33
FREE DAYS	34
COUNTRY ROAD	36
ANTICIPATION	37

CONTENTS
POEMS | TWO

BEFORE DAWN	39
MYSTICS	40
MY TEMPTATIONS	41
THE MODERN WORLD	42
GRAY	45
GUERNICA REVISITED	46
FOR EMILY D.	47
FAMILY OF ORIGIN	48
AN ANGEL	50
FROM MY WINDOW	51
BEWILDERMENT	52
GOD SHED HIS GRACE ON THEE	53
TREPIDATION ONCE REMOVED	54
SILENCE AMIDST THE DIN	56
THE FUNERAL	57
THE ART LESSON	58
CANYON'S EDGE	59

ONE

WHAT AM I MISSING?

I shave with Gillette Twin razor blades.
Ten bucks for a pack of ten
not sophisticated like the high-tech ones.
It's not about the money
nor the necessity to get with it.
You know, modernize.
My refrigerator does not make ice
it makes ice in a tray.
Living in the Jurassic period.
A luddite is unchangeable, unmoved.
Simplifying is not regression.
It's the stuff of new wave prose.
The coffee maker only makes coffee
it doesn't make ice cream.
One button.
Not a remote function.
It's the act of making it
not having it ready for you at 5 am.
I can't bake a fifteen-pound turkey
it won't fit in the oven.
Then again, you don't bake them often.
If the microwave goes
there goes my ability to melt butter.
It took years to replace Teflon pans.
I have found out too late
that they may cause cancer.
If gas powered mowers are banned,
What do I do?
I did get a battery powered blower
dragging around a 100' cord was getting tiresome.
The car is fifteen years old
beyond a CD player and AC
it's not very trail-blazing.
The TV is a 17-inch diagonal,
What the hell!
You can't see a flea on someone's ass.

No, but you can still see an ass.
I adjust the thermostat
it's getting a bit warmer.
I sip the unsweetened club soda
adjust the shade a bit
I hear a noise
it is the lawn service across the street,
it's getting louder.
The flowers in the pot
are exuberant and colorful.
Like looking out the window for the first time.

AWE AND WONDER

I cant stop thinking about it
a reverential feeling
that's supposed to overtake you.
You have to piece things together
especially if you're blind,
not absorbing the fascinating things around you.
There are two birds
splashing around in the birdbath
does that classify as awe?
You can practically watch a pole bean grow
six feet high from a seed
the size of your fingernail.
Wonder is a big deal
it puts you in a frame of mind
even if you view something unfamiliar.
Stick your hand in the ground
pull up a handful of potatoes or
peeling the skin off a dirty onion.
The wonder is in the ground
pretty much everywhere
you can touch stuff close to you.
We need to be reminded
of all the things we don't think about
awe and wonder is within reach.

TRAFFIC

I watch the traffic from the rear seat,
of an uncomfortable taxi.
It wasn't moving.
We were in a perpetual state of unrest.
The embedded odor from a thousand rides.
Is there a better option?
Uber has a sliding scale.
You can ride in a cheap dirty car,
for a lot less than a clean new car.
A taxi doesn't give you that option.
We are pitching replacement of gasoline.
Too much exhaust.
Too little relief.
I'm standing in a line of impatient parents.
Next to a line of idling vehicles.
They're not electric.
It's ok.
Sitting in air-conditioning while the earth heats up.
The air is not moving.
The temperature is high.
Breath in!
Buy an electric lawn mower.
It's a start.
If you like estimates, here's one.
There are an estimated 300 million vehicles in the USA.
There are 3.2 million EV's.
If that were a yearly production, it would take 85 years,
to replace all the internal combustion engines.
If we are in a hurry,
it's not looking good.
Still in the taxi.
My mind leaps across to the destination.
OK, lets think about an imponderable solution.
The radio is playing Rap.
Time to open the window.
Breath in!

DOUBT

This is an age of uncertainty.
We have arrived in a world where hubris,
has overtaken statesmanship and,
arrogance has replaced reason.
Years ago there was a PBS program.
It was titled, The Ascent of Man.
Jacob Bronowski, scientist, and philosopher,
was the host and writer.
We learned of man's technological innovation,
and great expansion of knowledge.
He ended the program at Auschwitz,
the infamous Nazi death camp.
Walking in what appeared to be a shallow swamp,
in ankle deep water,
he described the horrors of a regime,
that brought the world to its knees.
A destructive power,
that removed humanity from the right to be human.
He bent down and plunging his hand in the muck,
removed it dripping with detritus.
And proclaimed,' We must find a way to bring humanity
back to man'.
'We must touch people'.
With all the advantages we currently possess,
the privileges afforded and,
the opportunities we take for granted,
there is no guarantee that these assets
will protect you, from leadership.
Whose conviction is undiluted,
without regard of the feelings of others,
with absolute confidence and,
conviction that humanity needs to be controlled,
and brought to its knees,
and without recognition and acknowledgement,
the past will be dangerously repeated.

DELAY

I am working toward something useful
Like finishing a job I never started
But there are a lot of barriers moving forward
Birds dining happily in their feeder
Beans, dark green with tender pods producing in abundance
This, plus the sun casting a long shadow across the backyard.
In order to get started,
you have to overcome all these diversions.
Waiting for the coffee to perk.
A newspaper headline urging you to read.
Rain falling gently on the ledge,
and mist rising softly from the lawn.
These deflections aren't meant to confound
They're meant to remind you
That insects crawl under leaves
Flowers and foliage rustle in the wind
Pine trees sing when the wind blows
Daylilies bloom in the morning
That the room you're in is quiet and peaceful
And you love to give yourself useful advice
Like starting that job soon

MEASURING WITH A NEW SET OF RULES

You've got to start somewhere
I've been doing what I've been doing for a long time
Its had its ups and downs
So, I tell myself, What have I
Learned? Not so much patience
It's hard to have when you are trying to drive a point home
to a bunch of glassy-eyed workingmen.
It holds the same to the guy you are working for.
The question often comes up, Why did you do it that way?
Well, which way is that way?
I started a long time ago on my practice makes perfect.
It takes a lot not to be hasty or impetuous.
Are things supposed to get easier?
After 'X' amount of years of redundancy,
you find yourself with a smaller window of options
Another impending factor, forbearance.
Holding back from enforcing what is due or correct.
Passion is another dubious attribute.
Devotion to an activity, concept, object or cause.
Conveying that emotion in a non-condescending way
is a challenge.
Mister Rogers had a way of averting any possible slippage
into the disagreeable.
Used kindness and wonder to mitigate most of his distractions.
Can those attributes be applied to the work world?
To a client?
What sets one to respond in a manner of self-interest?
This isn't making a world to one's own specifications,
but it takes perseverance over patience to maintain
a sense of purpose.
Amid the chatter.
There are a lot of diverting forces.
Uncertainty in decision making.
Disregard for convention, compliance, consideration.
The opposite of excuse is indifference.
Why does Habitat for Humanity charge One hundred
sixty dollars to pick up junk?
Because they can.
Why does a job not finished or not well done, not matter?

Because it's not a matter of consideration.
For every 10% rise in the consumer price index,
there is a corresponding 10% decline in universal empathy,
Should I remain on guard?
Be more careful, more watchful,
against those who would ignore my directives.
Against those who choose not to have purpose.
Against those who fail to complete the task.
Is it better to take time, consider the miracles,
stick with kindness and wonder,
and move on.

CARDIAC REPERCUSSIONS

Lo, my heart beats frantically
When I wake up in the night

Like a bongo pounding ceaselessly
You're overcome with fright

When the beat begins to soften
You ponder the moments past

The darkness hovers over you
Thank God it didn't last

The walks you take are shortened
When you finally reach your gate

Glad that there's a bench to rest
To think about your fate

The mirror you're gazing into
Might not reveal your plight

Like feeling kind of restless
And giving up the fight

The cure is never certain
The advice not always wise

But adjusting how you make your way
May slacken your demise

ONE GLASS OR THREE

I drink too much wine, I know it
they know it, all the "they's" know it
but it doesn't show
not after three or four glasses
The Doc's are against it
so is the internet
I check it often and regularly
science says it kills you
even in moderation
Then there are the lucky ones
the yucks that live in Blue Zones
they eat, work, love and pray, all the time
and they drink wine, lots of it, pray tell
but they only drink the wine they make
My question, is it potent?
Well, it must be!
The average age for buying the farm is the mid-nineties
So, what is the operative call?
red or white
light and bright
acid or balanced
dry or nosy
Think about all those choices
everywhere you go
The nectar of the gods
they have a spigot and its always on.
It's so useful to our survival
that Jesus Christ claimed it was his blood.
You can think about hunger, thirst, energy and vitality.
sit at a table
look out at the moonlight
that meal you just ate tasted better
73 years old
Spring is wonderful.
the wine slithers down your throat
it's sending a message
Your doctor doesn't know you're drinking
Another glass?

EV MANDATE

In 2035 the US will stop producing gas powered cars
that's eleven years from now
Does it really matter?
It does to Elon Musk
it adds to the ongoing chorus
What demands will they make of us next?
Does everyone hear the same message?
Drive west and north from here
you witness varied and not so progressive places
fields, forests, farms, towns
and trucks
lots of them
they're not electric
keep driving
West Virginia is a good example of what ifs?
Like, what if you can no longer buy a regular car?
or, what if you can't afford an electric car?
Stop on a rural road off an interstate
check out the locals
buying chips, sodas and beer
they stand around the store sucking on coffin nails
have to smoke outside, what a disgrace
all the vehicles are trucks or late model gas guzzlers
as well as their clothes
tattoos on most of their exposed body parts
identity markings
the towns are all villes, Hockersville, Newville, Walkersville,
Hodgenville
rural roads with numbers like route 39, 41, 55
but progress is evident, lots of mobile phones
lottery tickets, racks of them.
Some are unemployed
they used to be coal miners
but coal, like other earth minerals
are no longer needed.
If lithium is discovered in Harlan County hill country
employment will rise
but same as coal
air and water pollution will follow

land destruction
dirty ground water
Can an automobile create a cultural change?
We cherish mobility
usually on our terms.
Forcing compliance is like forcing control
will there be a groundswell of revolt
Can you put a gun rack in an electric car?

LET'S START WITH THINGS THAT BOTHER YOU

Sorrow and compassion are a good place to start.
A lot of time can be spent pursuing elusive dreams.
You can assemble a lot of possessions,
because possessions for some,
compensate for things you don't have.
A book full of good pictures and paintings,
it can bring a certain solitude.
Because, you can view them vicariously,
experiencing in the imagination,
through the actions or images of others.
Maybe we all tend to do this.
So many share the fate of an artist, poet or architect.
Because, each day,
assuming you are leading a creative life,
often with a new hope,
A new challenge,
A new opportunity.
You seek confirmation through validation.
It is good to maintain some compassion for what you do?
For the act of creating,
and the hope,
somewhat elusive,
that it will bring some joy to the recipient,
the viewer,
the participant.
And there is faith in reflection.
Just as there is value in dreaming.
Does all the stuff,
and all the acts,
and all the product assembled,
equal to the sum of its parts?
Is it better to collect then discard.
It confirms the pattern of late recognition.
If you're good at what you do,
It's good to leave some residue.
What you leave behind
is not so much a legacy,
as it is a reminder.

ENERGY

I think I'm from another time.
That's a fact.
Not factual.
Imagine hanging around with Robert Rauschenberg,
in the late 1950's,
when you could buy a canvas from him,
for the change in your pocket.
Playing poker in the wee hours, with John Cage,
de Koening and a host of others.
Or watching Motherwell stroke paint on canvases.
Serendipity and spontaneity were the external forces.
No apologies.
No excuses.
Just irreverence and banter.
Intellectual,
Without superiority,
authority or prestige.
Every idea was a new idea. Technology was not predominate.
Do creative types get together and drink?
The crossover talent show was remarkable.
Collaborations of artists, poets, musicians, critics and cads.
More the norm than the exception.
Eventually, with all that controlled energy,
Something would happen.
Something would give.
Expression turned into emotion.
Emotion turned into rebellion.
Rebellion turned into chaos.
Chaos brought forth resistance.
There was a feeling,
perhaps universal,
that we were in this together.
The ART of resistance, brought forth the certainty,
There was something we knew about,
Psychology, ecology, economics, technology, nature,
birds, love and,
the emerging evils of capitalism.
It colored our thinking.
We draped ourselves in the US flag.

It made us tough.
Ready to challenge authority,
Ready to make change.
Without the tools to construct it.
What is unnerving,
but to some degree reassuring,
is all this turmoil is remembered as romantic.
Imagine that!
We dispelled the notion that creativity and capitalism,
were mutually exclusive,
But in reality,
creativity is a byproduct of capitalism.
Imagine that, again!

THE BAKERY LINE

I stand in line
With doubt and wonder
How long the wait may be

It doesn't end
I stare out straight
As far as I can see

I should have brought
Along with me
Some biscuits and some tea

But I never thought
The wait would be
As long as it seems to me

Should patience play
A modest role
As time keeps ticking by

Or should I just remove myself
And try another time

It's not that I'm that hungry
Nor do I need to eat

But if the line picked up a bit
I shan't be on the brink

But all this time is justified
By those that had their fill

For me I can't be mollified
To miss this luscious thrill

Checking time before you come
Seems to be the key

It would have helped my sweet desire
But it never dawned on me

A SHORT TRIP

I was riding with my dad
an old Rambler Ambassador.
He bought them old
maybe for a 100 bucks.
Can't recall the destination.
I had the radio on
the window vent was open
so he could blow out his smoke.
Barry Mcquire came on the radio
Eve of Destruction.
He was singing a lament;
he seemed to have a lot of grief.
I said, Dad, Vietnam is not a good war.
No wars are good was the reply.
Do you think there will be trouble in America?
America is never in trouble.
Need to think about yourself
and where you are going.
The road took a hard right
Dad sucked on his cigarette.
We stopped for gas.
I got a coke;
he got some Camels, no filters.

HEAT

It's 95 degrees outside
85 in the shade
the air doesn't move.
Bugs fly around, frenzied
birds aren't very active
heat has a presence.
It surrounds you like a heavy coat
word is, it's getting worse
100 degrees, 90 in the shade.
Is it hotter than the chain gang crew
chopping weeds in Cool Hand Luke.
Geeze it was hot.
Is all this theorizing?
That the earth is burning up
no turning back.
Lots of folks, mostly southern,
wrote about heat.
Carson Mccullers, Flannery O'Conner, Tennessee Williams.
Very sweaty times
you tend to expect what you're told
look at temperature records.
In 1898 it reached 100 degrees
apparently more than once
now we are setting records yearly.
If you didn't know better
we'll soon be boiling water on the sidewalk
that's not fun.
But if you weren't bombarded
with constant temperature updates
would you just assume
that summers are HOT.
Like they've always been
wear shorts, take cover
and hang around near water.

ARISE AND REFLECT

You're waiting for morning
sun to rise, first light
even though it's still before 5 am.
Too early for coffee
but not for some meditation
just as the light emerges.
You peek at the shapes in the garden
some reflecting early light
a bird perches on the feeder.
This is what you have been planning
everything complete and finished
your hand rubs your cheek.
What happened years ago?
When you strolled through beautiful gardens
contemplating one of your own.
You looked at fine gravel
stones, bricks and rock
cascading flowers of brilliance.
Setting yourself to work
you made what you thought
would be a tribute to these places.
You've been fascinated with growing your own
turning earth and planting seeds
eating the bounty.
All this because you saw this as a journey
not a conclusion.
You want to say, so what.
The coffee is now perking
the sun has risen.
Surely, all of this was worth it.

DECIPHERING THE CHATTER

Crime is rising in my city.
Is it perceived or real?
The mix of people hasn't changed
I noticed tire marks on the street
that must tell you something.
The sidewalks
could use some TLC
but this isn't Europe,
where the shopkeeper sweeps.
If perception is reality
Do you need a bulletproof vest?
There are some shady characters,
carry change.
Very few empty storefronts,
that says healthy.
The last time I read about crime
It was a 2 am incident.
That tells you something.
What are you doing at 2 am
on an empty city street.
If you keep moving your head
left and right
it makes your neck hurt.
But it makes you safer.
Or, just stop reading bad news.

WAR DEBT

WWII ended 79 years ago.
I was born five years later.
My father died in 1980.
He was a WWII veteran.
I grew up on a street in Pittsburgh
with row houses barely five feet apart.
We lived next door to Mrs. Gavins,
A kind old lady who had a son.
Her son was always there.
He stood like a sentinel, barely moving,
next to the window in the living room
partly hidden by the curtain.
I wanted to ask Mrs. Gavins about him,
but I was afraid.
I did ask my mother.
she said he had a bad time in the war.
My parents were fluent in German.
They would often converse
to conceal their discussion from their children.
My father was born in Germany.
He arrived shortly after WWI.
His family, like so many others left
to put behind devastation and despair.
I once asked my father
why he didn't teach his children German.
His reply, without emotion,
Americans don't like Germans or Germany.
My father served in the 106th infantry.
One of the last large deployments in the war.
Their Division was consigned upon arrival
to attack the German advance in Hurtgen forest.
The offense known as the Battle of the Bulge.
It began on December 9, 1944.
There were 75,000 casualties and
20,000 deaths.
What I gleaned from my father was
little of his military service.
As a child I didn't realize he had trouble
talking about the war.

Perhaps, like so many soldiers
he carried his discomfort throughout his life.
Never realizing there may have been a path to recovery.
I visited this battlefield numerous times
through history books and photographs.
The battle was fought in the dead of winter.
He said the trigger on his rifle would freeze
so, you had to continuously fire it.
They did not remove their boots
for over a month for fear of freezing their feet.
When they did remove them, their skin
was adhered to their socks.
After weeks of shelling,
the allies broke through the enemy lines.
They were fighting old men and children.
Prisoners were taken, both sides.
The Americans contained them.
The Germans killed them.
My father stayed on after the war with a transition team.
He spoke German.
He didn't last long.
No stomach for the devastation.
So little is known about the temperament
of the returning GI's.
It seems, the countenance of today's military
Is to bestow honor without sacrifice.
The history of the great war
passed over thousands of veterans
who fought with valor and distinction.
So, what do I make of this?
I think a lot of veterans came home from the war
and fell through the cracks.
No safety nets.
Little preparation to reunite with family.
They were as distant to solving mental problems
as the war is distant today.
Now, over forty years after my fathers death
I am certain
my fathers life was a web of insecurity,
vacillation and uncertainty.
A confounding and perplexing
state of mind.
That haunted him throughout his life.

NEWS

There were 12 negative articles
in the newspaper today.
Trouble spots all over.
North Korea is dropping feces
on South Korea.
Tiawan appears to be surrounded.
Defense lines look weak in Ukraine.
Airlines are grounded.
Some are pissing off customers.
Hail as large as baseballs pulverize Texas.
Tornados bounce around the Midwest
like rubber balls.
This is just a start.
Private Equity is buying up America.
Banks lament the disappearance of
publicly held companies.
Not to mention fires
raging in the west, midwest,
forests and prairies.
Cicadas are wreaking havoc.
Did the bible predict this?
We are having an election in November
Along with an insurrection?
This is the dark side.
On the bright side
The sun arrived at 5:45 this am.
The temperature was cool
birds came around
lots of clatter.
A few dogs barking.
There was a breeze.
And other than being a little warm
it will likely be a pretty nice day.
This proves there is a parallel universe.
The one we occupy
and the one that perpetuates
an ongoing mantra
of disappointing news.
This universe is uninhabitable.

The sun is rising
sky is pink.
Take that as positive news.

SO LONG FRANK LIOYD WRIGHT

Simon and Garfunkel sang a song
titled, So Long Frank Lloyd Wright.
Why were they saying, so long?
Wright hasn't gone anywhere.
He is a multi-million dollar
cottage industry.
You can buy his stuff everywhere.
Let's face it
the marketing geniuses
co-opted his image and reputation.
Wright likely saw the potential of his
marketing potential
in the early 1950's.
His career skyrocketed after
the opening of the Johnon Wax headquarters in
Racine, Wisconsin, and
on the heels of Fallingwater
the consummate twentieth century residence.
His status rose to the greatest architect
of the twentieth century.
Americas greatest contribution
to his art form.
Put all these accolades aside.
You need to see his stuff.
Start a hundred plus years ago
and travel through the mid 1950's.
The range is ball-busting.
How did he do all this?
Who helped him?
And now, nearly 66 years after his death
he's a folk hero.
Misunderstood, maligned, and sometimes defamed,
but, not without an acquired reverence.
As revisionist history goes
we revisit to find relevance
sometimes to find comfort
sometimes to find ourselves.
Not necessarily to pinpoint
our shortcomings.

But more so, a few willful–
not marginalized – people realize
that Wright invented or improved more stuff
than you can catalog,
from cross-ventilation to carports
geo-thermal energy to low-cost housing
solar orientation to thermal insulation.
It's best to stop now
before you run out of breath.
But, not before noting his visionary ideas
birthed the modern-day ranch house.
One might ask, Why do we go backward,
before we go forward?
Wright once said,
An Architect isn't made so much,
by way of a brain,
but more so by a cultured and enriched heart.
Go figure.
Let's start a list,
Who has a cultured and enriched heart today?
When you get to zero, you figured it out.
You got to look hard, real hard
to find this attribute today
in politics, in entertainment, in sports
the list goes on.
Back to Wright.
One of his clients said to him
in the early 1900's
that they were looking for an architect
to design a home for them.
They informed Mr. Wright that they came to him
because he exhibited a refined and principled
countenance.
Think about that for a while.
So long, Frank Lloyd Wright.

SKY

The sky is blue
brilliant, right before
the haze sets in.
It's the heat
starts in June
hangs around and intensifies
until August.
The better months are
May and September.
You sweat less.
Your hand reaches
for a clippers.
You want to do something.
A helicopter approaches
It's deafening
The hospital is a mile away.
Urban noise.
I've looked at this yard
for years.
There's not much to do
in heat.
Not much for me to do.
A few clouds arrive.
Relief, relief.

THINKING ABOUT ANXIETY

My index finger
is jammed in a poetry book
on page 92.
It's a poem about smoking, drinking and
a donkey.
None of which I know much about
except drinking
in moderation.
I close my eyes
an image appears in my head.
I'm in an airplane
on a tarmac waiting interminably
while lightning and thunder
pound the fuselage.
It brings on instant anxiety.
The same effect overtakes me
when I have to do something
I don't want to do.
Like buy a car
or argue about children.
I scribble a few notes to myself
if only to relieve
my wandering thoughts.
There is a lot of subject matter.
Like getting lost in the country
because the sun wasn't shining
and you couldn't tell
north from south.
Doubtful subject matter.
It's getting late
too much time has passed.
The doorbell rings
as a package hits the stoop.
A break from the solitude
The phone rings
I don't want to answer it.
One more thing I don't want to do.

CHILDHOOD

I'm looking at a photo of my father
with four of his children.
They stand to his right
tallest to the far right
descending like steps to the shortest.
We look like Russian nesting dolls.
He has on a white tee-shirt.
It's tight, and his muscles ripple.
We have the additional appearance of
scrawny street urchins.
Most likely
hand me down clothes.
It's a poor quality
black and white photo.
Most likely made with a
Brownie camera.
There is a burning cigarette
in my father's left hand.
He always had a cigarette in his hand
or one hanging from his lips.
Hard to remember where we were.
But, if it was a summer weekend
we were in a state park
not too far from home.
My mom took the picture
she always took them
because she was rarely in
any picture.
We probably spent the rest of the afternoon
tumbling around
in a big field of grass.
But I don't remember.
I really can't remember.
All these photos
draw blanks.
You scratch your chin
say what the hell.
It must have been fun.
I know it was fun.

BOOKS

I'm looking at boxes
piled high in a corner.
They are overflowing
and too heavy to lift.
They are full of books
big books
art books.
I thought I needed them.
That's why I had them
supplementing my career.
The career is ending.
The books, endless.
Boy, I thought
I needed them.
Full of stuff I aspired to.
A little late now.
They're just for a coffee table.
Bookshelves look great
in photographs.
They make a room look
intelligent
livable.
The ones without pictures
novels
fiction and non-fiction.
Not as heavy to move.
They say you can tell a person's IQ
by the number of books in a room.
Book collecting
is like meditation
they create a calming environment
spark recognition
enhance memory.
But someday
sooner or later
they will need to find
a new place to live.
Someone else's problem.
They may still have a value

too you.
And value aligns with
behavior.
You conduct yourself differently
in a room full of books.

STATE OF THE WORLD

The disruptions defy expectations
radiant heat lights up the night
stars quiver through a veiled haze
warm water rolls over
once cold rocks
flowers wilt at the first
sight of sunlight
vines entwine the tallest trees.
When is the day of reckoning?
Who noticed the fall of Icarus?
It escaped our grasp.
If extremes are the new normal,
the operating model of the future,
can we find a shady spot?
You can run
but you cannot hide
this is widely known.
The mantra seems to be
escape to high ground.
You can see your years
feel your years
feel your time
Closing in on you.

FREE DAYS

Passing time each day
it wasn't supposed to be
like this.
Watching flowers grow
that's what it's called.
You can imagine
you are somewhere else
driving through a forest or
drinking coffee.
The help looks distracted, timid.
What's next?
a hardware store from 1900
a church without a steeple.
When you come back to where you left
from your couch
you drift into another
aimless wandering.
I went on what was
supposed to be
an unforgettable trip.
You enjoyed the view
stopped to gaze
the arrival, uneventful.
Mingling and co-mingling.
Looking for a place to park
in the shade.
A two-liter bottle of
water would help.
When you show up
does anyone miss you
even if you're there.
Every event was a non-event.
You get fidgety in your seat
while a hot wind blows the trees.
Expecting exceptional
it is reduced to average.
I roll my eyes
waiting impatiently
for things to improve.

For the earth to stop spinning.
I realize
I have lots of time
free time.
Free days.
It wasn't supposed to be
like this.

COUNTRY ROAD

The road transverses pastoral fields
nestled in a V-shaped valley
forests roll-up the shallow hills
black and white shadows
pattern the green canvas.
We are driving in a
sparsely populated local
unaltered and resistive
to any modern intervention.
Your eyes roam
with pensive inquiry
you're answered back with
complacency, as if
the landscape is unconcerned.
Grey clouds form, threatening rain
they float under deep azure sky.
A few raindrops fall
instantly, absorbed and evaporated.
This is the world, green and blue.
Two colors, not black and white.
Unchanged, not anachronistic
This intrusion is temporary.
A deer stands heedless
on the side of the road.
as if to gesture to me
You'll be leaving soon.

ANTICIPATION

I'm waiting anxiously, can only stare at the walls
thinking about the call up
the tiny room with all the monitors.
There is a lead -up here
it's been a year in coming
watching how you live and how you eat.
The room is dark, with a low hum
you hook up to a monitor
you can hear the tear on the IV needle pack.
Next is all small performance
needle in, IV in, dye in
step on the treadmill.
Start slow and awkward
speed increases, incline rises
blood pressure rising.
All this to let you know
you're ok, or not ok.
So, what are the results?
You'll find out in a day or two
after the doc looks it over
all this to keep your ticker, ticking.

TWO

BEFORE DAWN

Dark the passage, dark the path
glimmering beads thru cobwebbed branches.
Forms and faces profiled on compacted leaves
footsteps, nearly silent,
alien sounds preceding sunrise.
Abstract shapes designed by darkness,
variegated shades of black,
the comforting resonance of still dripping water.
Embrace this solitude of obsidian-grey wetness
Cave-like, womb-like, before light.

MYSTICS

Their voices ring with inflected sound
Like moistened weather, eastern bound;
Scenarios that stretch my rambling spirit,
Discovering my past in a lost and found.
They cite with clever anecdote
The fears you hide inside your cloak;
Plucking low-hung deficiencies,
And surround your head like wisping smoke.
Reach deeply into your layered soul
Like puzzle pieces then made whole;
Are you enlightened or merely disengaged,
Is the struggle for comfort all push and pull.
Can our future be so handily foretold
Like merchandise first bought, then sold;
As you listen with rapt attentive regard,
Predictions that often leave you cold.
But fear of what's unknown can be
A path to blindness or a light to see;
These words can relinquish hidden dismay,
Like a burden removed, set free, set free.

MY TEMPTATIONS

Grass is greener though I despair,
I'm in retraction, sensing needs,
Yet life retreats into thin air
Though others said just plant a seed
On pretense and passions I must feed;
Perhaps a long unbroken sleep;
Courage, face the daunting task,
Imprudent actions wild and rash,
These thoughts resound submerged and deep.

THE MODERN WORLD

Here we go again
one more headline castigating
the towering inferno
of greed
Repentance is not
advisable
all actions are not
regrettable
the volume of apologies
receding.
Awash in noxious banter,
billowing surges
of blame
take pride in our
universal good.
Heed the rhetoric
the advice is hackneyed
drown in mundane
guidance
find comfort in
collective misery.
Turn to sources
of consolation
ply the Samaritan's trade
there is solace,
in prayer.
They aren't thine enemies,
they reflect our
grief and despair
undaunted, they proceeded
unaware.
There are endless miles
of reasons
the system is fraught
with aberrations
damn the wisdom
consume the vice.
Be honest, be firm
equivocate

the intentions were always noble
the results garnered
mixed reviews.
Opinions trump sound persuasion
the information need not be
revealed
fastidious is the
informant.
The minions awash in red ink
it is not the color
of money
it is more the color of
resignation.
Hope as imbibed
springs eternal
the elixir of emancipation,
liberty
to feel without reproach.
The sinister nature of those
that control
leadership grants immunity for
the demi-gods
of undeserved enterprise.
Separation of church and state
the stable foundation
of democracy
is it really just separation
from them and us?
Empowered to legally suffer
and authorization to all,
to invest in oneself
any consequences merely the result
of ignorance.
The net spread wide
with discontent
malfeasance pursued is a
cherished diploma
unchallenged, unorthodox, unpunished.
Impertinence is the disease

of the uninformed
it's Monday morning, go to work
or go to work on
collective concrescence.
Ordained into a culture of
default as we seek relevance in daily chaos
and here we go,
again.

GRAY

Gray is the color of contrition.
It is the color of complaint.
It removes all other colors
by neutralizing brightness;
it clings to a surface
like sap to a tree.
Unforgiving it renders life
dull and displaced.
Gray is the color of repentance,
It is the color of necessity.
It creates a natural compulsion
to surrender and,
devoid of nuance, complexion is compromised
It is a pigmentation
that insinuates regret.
Gray is the color of sorrow.
It is seasonal, just as life is fluxuating.
It repudiates all the chromatic
intensity of the color spectrum.
Rendering inconsolable grief,
it blankets desire.
It implies a sense of loss,
and a longing to renew.
Gray is the color of suggestion.
It paints dull our mood and outlook.
It is the achromatic
base line without hue,
reflecting light without dispersion.
It is temporal and, prompts us to awaken.
It is an entrée to act.
Gray is the color of change.

GUERNICA REVISITED

Twisted, achromatic we view these tortured forms,
Compelled to stare yet turn away;
The blue-black harshness of a thunderstorm,
Knotted torsos, wounded figures, shocking interplay;
Carbon objects, clothed in gray, pressed hard with glaring white,
Grief, disaster, shrieking beasts, project a gruesome sight,
Forms that weep with shock and pain, consumes you with its might,
Immense and vast, chaotic strife: transmit, impart, convey.
With a brilliance unconstrained, it strikes to illustrate,
The wreckage and distortion of war;
Silent screams, host agony, the urge to irritate,
Its violent impact radiates, and shakes us to the core;
Naked and dazed, we withdraw ourselves, raging with our hate,
This is art, and when its truth, comfort it negates,
Yet brings to light, despite indifference, the passion to create,
Now praise this morbid artistry, it brings pathos to the fore.

FOR EMILY D.

I sense the world is slowing down
I feel it in my feet,
From a family stubborn, dogma bred
That prides itself on biased retreat.
And see a close to everything
Dead ends, dark withered forms;
Sprung from a chilly stern neglect
I witness black impending storms.
A mood that's sullen, dim and stark
Chases fast away the light,
I came about this disposition.
By turning tail, with fevered fright.
With such uncertain steps, I pause,
And endure my trepidation;
Timid, weak and spiritless
Has this dread become my life's vocation?

FAMILY OF ORIGIN

I remember, though hazy,
the meanderings of a small child.
Dutifully listening to demands
responding fitfully, or indifferently.
Seeming small in a small house,
the daunting height of the staircase.
Narrow halls with many doors,
small windows with dismal light.
Doors that were open
doors that were closed.
Furniture tightly packed
little room for movement.
Small cardboard boxes
things collected, my stuff.
A small window with a
narrow view to a narrow alley.
The house stood like a soldier
on the street, all uniform in color.
All concrete, no grass,
beyond the yard, intimidating.
Inaccessible and terrifying,
I was safe inside.
Sibling rivalry or disinterested siblings
I sought isolation.
Piled together on a sofa,
piled together in a car.
One tricycle, one bike
hard tires or flat tires.
The house creaked and moaned
the wind made it rattle.
Four siblings, two brothers, two sisters,
Thrown together, go out and play.
Packed like eggs in a carton
packed in the back seat of the car.
Dinner always spread thin
Leftovers, three times a week.
Walking to school
the longest three blocks imaginable.
Always a journey, a small boy's fear

big school doors, not my bedroom.
Nuns in black habits
towering, demanding, overbearing.
A small boy in a big classroom
hiding behind my big desk, am I invisible?
Always singled out, always questioned
Are you with us? Discipline followed.
The dread of self-imposed failure
I disliked the place, I disliked their face.
Restrained in the playground, like my yard
enclosed with a spike rail fence.
What seemed like a regular occurrence,
Parents meeting with the nuns.
Quiet, nervous, fidgeting in the anteroom
Awaiting the outcome.
Once again, not applying myself
Once again, extended time in my bedroom
School, church, rectory,
they remain a vivid graphic memory.
Grey windows, black roofs,
Cold bricks and stained concrete.
A tableau of silence
a stage of still and motionless objects.
I wanted to be a talisman,
Holding onto my rabbit's foot.
I imagined being a giant
Looking down on these buildings.
I wanted to have special powers
or special protection.
How could I fit in, is fear
like awkwardness, permanent or reoccurring?
I continue to seek resolve, years pass.
Looking back, where is my sanctuary?
A refuge, asylum, a holy place?
Step out of the dark, into the light.

AN ANGEL

I felt a presence rest on me,
A seraph whispers in;
With a serenade well pitched and prim,
Alerting me of sin.
A disguise removed, I open up,
A sound I need to hear;
Then felt the soft ephemeral voice,
Persuasive and sincere.
Serene the murmur cooed quietly,
A message for my soul;
Dispatched with sound efficiency,
While beseeching self-control.
These words were meant to carry forth,
A pitch to comprehend;
I embraced them with sagacity,
Lest my mask makes me pretend.

FROM MY WINDOW

The window in my quiet room,
Frames a still reality
From autumn rust to verdant June.
Perched upon a rigid chair,
I view a polychromed schematic
With folded arms, I sit alone and stare.
This portal to the world beyond,
Absorbed in pensive observation
To my sense of being, I willfully respond.
It's from this vantage, I observe,
So safe and calm within
An intimate surrounding, silent, well preserved.
Yet I imagine, beyond this stage,
The world envelopes all
And I prefer to sit alone, inside this peaceful cage.
This window in my quiet room,
Bestows a chosen reality
Providing repose and solitude
It's a refuge not a tomb.

BEWILDERMENT

I sit with aged restlessness
buried in my toil;
I wonder at reflected light,
and mulch upon the soil.
Concrete cracks and crater pits
holes that fill the field;
I contemplate these random seams,
like layers split and peeled.
Leaves once brilliant, now deceased
frigid air more like a torch;
has claimed the life of verdant green,
nature's awe inspiring force.
I ponder views so close at hand
their presence piercing and cold;
these modest scenes reveal themselves,
minute, but a thrill to behold.

GOD SHED HIS GRACE ON THEE

We ponder the clogged and crowded highways.
Eroded hills, like skins of prunes, wrinkled, furrowed
and creased.
We weep?
Air that stifles as we inhale, heat with pressure, unrelieved.
Colorless grey, forests in retreat, fractured, broken,
lifeless bark.
We weep?
Species toil for survival, extinction awaits the weak.
Habitats vanishing, parched and arid, dusty plains,
a trace of verdant past.
We weep?
Water rising angrily, consumes with vapid ease.
Forest succumb, menaced by machines, mangle,
claw and decimate.
We weep?
Mineral scars, crevices deep, wounds without a suture -
black water.
Spilling and staining, tenaciously, with imperishable
strength and grip.
We weep?
The goo that power our machines, guerilla tactics subdue us.
Implements control, discarded after hasty use, indifferent,
callous, vain.
We turn?
The talons of excessive will, emboldened in its path.
Fearless determination, rushing to careless advance,
pitiless, unaware of consequences.
We turn?
The faithful speaking piety, others preach restraint.
Choose wisely, information blankets all, confused,
engulfed and unprepared.
We'll learn?

TREPIDATION ONCE REMOVED

Reflection is not a chosen route,
If not accustomed to this path;
Circumstances take control,
I stroke my brow, or avoid this task.
What then is disregarded,
And what is meant to keep;
Piled like kindling, odds and ends,
My stacks of books compete.
Questions circle aimlessly,
Random texts with titles, thick and thin,
Do they impart a silent repetition,
Or a chatty, conversant and noisy din.
I imagine things that don't exist,
And wonder vicariously;
Submerged in places, near and far,
Careless thoughts that weary me.
Replace these notions with vigor, bold,
Sense an awakening, not reprieve;
The outward goals are near at hand
Yet arduous to conceive.
Prepare for moments, unfulfilled,
Beckoning with distant, suggestive calls;
Entrapment is a force of will
Cower, then uncertainty casts a pall.
Trapped or free, I ponder,
Wallow, stuck in dry embrace;
Inside my space, oppressed and dim,
A darkened path I face?
Is the door ajar and accessible,
Does it re-open with purpose or cause;
Or must one wait and contemplate,
Does a custodian make you pause.
As I foster feelings trite or brave,
Like a wind that makes a chill;
Are feelings that stray without purpose,
Reckless, vain or still.
Haunted at once by omens,
A failure to portend.
With a rolling mind and capricious whims

Often powerless to defend.
Years like days or seconds pass,
Persistence of vision inclines;
The books are stacked haphazardly,
No more rules or orders assigned.
Are you on your own; and with yourself,
Are you cornered by odious chimes;
Do you churn with stifled rectitude,
Discordant with your own sense of time.
Are we a structure like a building,
With its bones and teeth and skin;
That suggest, a sense of permanence,
Your life effects, stored safe within.

SILENCE AMIDST THE DIN

You are alone
You are alone, more than you think.
One-half of your life
Is a dream state.
Alone with your thoughts
Alone in a car, on a bus, on a walk.
Solitude can be enfolding
Isolation can be intoxicating
But it has tentacles,
Or is it a many-headed hydra?
Seclusion begets turmoil.
Multiple thoughts are feelings unrequited.
Correspondence of intentions, without reason
Expectations, limited by frustration
Sometimes internal passions are fueled -
By possibilities
Perceptions, fraught with uncertainty
Can you share these inner journeys?
Is most of it made up, in your head
Or is reality a game of hide-and-seek?

THE FUNERAL

In a blended refrain
They praised this great man,
Who rarely veered from the center,
And lived large by a plan.
Moved more by the truth of myth
Rather than off act,
When the righteous were summoned,
He never failed to react.
Bearing his course of influence
He fought grief and despair,
And abided by rapture,
With a well-spring of prayer.
Driven by dogma
He lived by the 1vord,
Regale in your beliefs,
Lest you'll never be heard.
With a hegemony embodied
He sought strength to lead,
Condescending to the crestless,
With an authoritative creed.
As the scriptures entreat
Our need to address,
The flaws that we live with,
Each loath to confess.
He passed into vapor
As the word imputed our guilt,
We're all woven together,
Like a bric-a-brac quilt.
Look into the mirror
And accept our improbable fate.
The only way of the righteous,
Is to wipe clean the slate.

THE ART LESSON

Our houses of art are sometimes ubiquitous
but often daring or restrained,
where inquisitive minds are never barred,
often times vexing, so let down your guard,
and to some the pleasure, comes very hard.
These are places for contemplative minds, the only request -
unrestricted time.
No prior condition nor approval committed,
but engaging your impulse is always permitted.
Cultivated variations displaying color and line,
layers of texture, multi-dimensions defined,
permeation of our senses, raised to the sublime.
Truth and beauty we often debate
yet it doesn't diminish out power to create.
These shrines represent both belief and desire,
rise up from the ordinary, stimulate and inspire.
Art is expressive of our highest ideals
transformative, enlightening, our potential revealed.

CANYON'S EDGE

I stand in reverence to the power of place,
Imposing and daunting, yet I covet its grace,
Colors flamboyant, pressed folds of the earth.
Distances retreat, in lines hard to conceive
No beginning or end, you abandon the search.
Here from this vantage, sense millenniums past
Eons of stories carved in its brow
This earth formed monument, destined to last;
One ponders how massive and mighty its source.
That carved and incised with such brutal force,
The rim of the horizon matches the grand billowed sky
While emotions are mingled with wonder and awe.
Like a deity worshipped, its presence on high
This canyon so grand, casts us humble and small.

www.ingramcontent.com/pod-product-compliance
Lightning Source LLC
Chambersburg PA
CBHW061810070526
44586CB00024B/2797